W9-AYF-185

11/13

Fascinating INSECTS

Grasshoppers

Aaron Carr

www.av2books.com

LET'S READ
AV²
BY WEIGL™
ADDED VALUE • AUDIO VISUAL

Go to **www.av2books.com**, and enter this book's unique code.

BOOK CODE

J150157

AV² by Weigl brings you media enhanced books that support active learning.

AV² provides enriched content that supplements and complements this book. Weigl's AV² books strive to create inspired learning and engage young minds in a total learning experience.

Your AV² Media Enhanced books come alive with...

Audio
Listen to sections of the book read aloud.

Video
Watch informative video clips.

Embedded Weblinks
Gain additional information for research.

Try This!
Complete activities and hands-on experiments.

Key Words
Study vocabulary, and complete a matching word activity.

Quizzes
Test your knowledge.

Slide Show
View images and captions, and prepare a presentation.

... and much, much more!

Published by AV² by Weigl
350 5th Avenue, 59th Floor New York, NY 10118
Website: www.av2books.com   www.weigl.com

Library of Congress Control Number: 2013937273
ISBN 978-1-62127-328-8 (hardcover)
ISBN 978-1-62127-333-2 (softcover)

Printed in the United States of America in North Mankato, Minnesota
1 2 3 4 5 6 7 8 9 0 17 16 15 14 13

052013
WEP040413

Project Coordinator: Aaron Carr   Art Director: Terry Paulhus

Weigl acknowledges Getty Images as the primary image supplier for this title.

Grasshoppers

CONTENTS

Meet the grasshopper.

Grasshoppers are small insects.
They can be many different colors.

Grasshoppers can be found
all around the world.

All around the world,
grasshoppers live in fields and forests.

Grasshoppers are born when they hatch from eggs.

When they hatch from eggs, grasshoppers are very small.

Grasshoppers have long legs.

With very long legs,
grasshoppers can jump very far.

Grasshoppers have two large eyes.

With two large eyes,
grasshoppers can see all around them.

Grasshoppers have two pairs of wings.

14

With two pairs of wings,
grasshoppers fly from place to place.

Grasshoppers rub their legs
and wings together.

By rubbing their legs and wings together,
grasshoppers can make sounds.

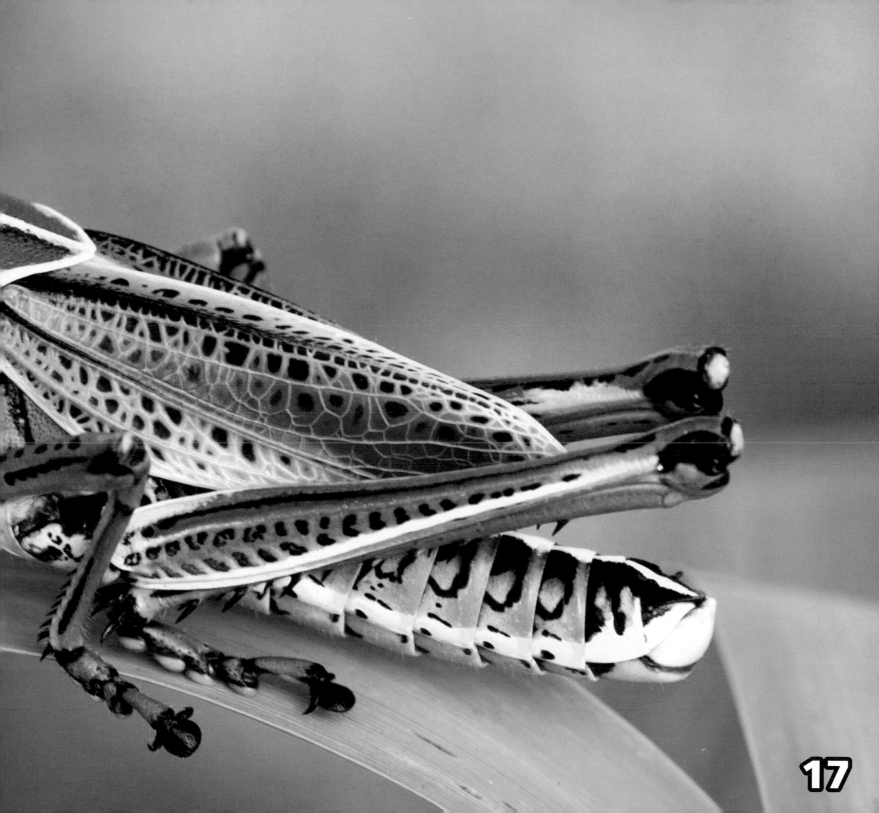

17

Grasshoppers eat plants.

Eating plants gives grasshoppers everything they need to be healthy.

Grasshoppers are important in nature.

In nature,
grasshoppers help keep plants healthy.

GRASSHOPPER FACTS

These pages provide more detail about the interesting facts found in the book. They are intended to be used by adults as a learning support to help young readers round out their knowledge of each insect or arachnid featured in the *Fascinating Insects* series.

Pages 4–5

Grasshoppers are insects. Insects have six jointed legs and hard shells, or exoskeletons, with three parts: the head, thorax, and abdomen. Holes in the thorax, called spiracles, let grasshoppers breathe. There are more than 10,000 species of grasshoppers. They can be 0.4 to 4 inches (1 to 11 centimeters) long. Females are often larger than males. Grasshoppers may be green, olive, red, brown, or black. They sometimes have yellow or green markings.

Pages 6–7

Grasshoppers can be found all around the world. They live in a wide variety of habitats around the world. Grasshoppers can be found on all continents except Antarctica. They live in tropical and temperate forests, grasslands, and even steppe areas near deserts. Some grasshoppers have adapted to special habitats. One species of South American grasshopper lives on floating plants and even swims to lay its eggs.

Pages 8–9

Grasshoppers are born when they hatch from eggs. Grasshopper eggs are laid in the summer and hatch the following spring. Newly hatched grasshoppers are called nymphs. They look like adult grasshoppers, but they are small and do not have wings. In 5 to 10 days, nymphs grow larger and molt, or shed their skin, 5 to 6 times. By 30 days, the wings have formed, and the grasshopper is an adult.

Pages 10–11

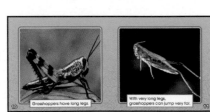

Grasshoppers have very long legs. The grasshopper's hind legs are adapted for jumping. The upper part of the hind legs has large, powerful muscles that allow the grasshopper to jump great distances. A grasshopper can jump about 20 times the length of its body. When grasshoppers walk, they use all six legs.

KEY WORDS

Research has shown that as much as 65 percent of all written material published in English is made up of 300 words. These 300 words cannot be taught using pictures or learned by sounding them out. They must be recognized by sight. This book contains 43 common sight words to help young readers improve their reading fluency and comprehension. This book also teaches young readers several important content words. These words are paired with pictures to aid in learning and improve understanding.

Page	Sight Words First Appearance
4	the
5	are, be, can, different, many, small, they
7	all, and, around, found, in, live, world
8	from, when
9	very
10	have, long
11	far, with
12	eyes, large, two
13	see, them
14	of
15	from, place, to
16	by, make, sounds, their, together
18	eat, plants
19	gives, need
20	help, important, keep

Page	Content Words First Appearance
4	grasshopper
5	colors, insects
7	fields, forests
8	eggs
10	legs
14	pairs, wings
20	nature